CROW'S SHELLS

Artistic Basketry of Puget Sound

CROW'S SHELLS

Artistic Basketry of Puget Sound

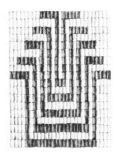

Nile Thompson and Carolyn Marr

*Prepared for the Skokomish Indian Tribe
with support from the Folk Arts Program
of the National Endowment for The Arts*

DUSHUYAY PUBLICATIONS
Seattle, Washington

ISBN: 0-9611586-0-3

DUSHUYAY PUBLICATIONS
751 North 75th Street
Seattle, Washington 98103

Contents

Acknowledgements

This catalog accompanies a series of exhibits sponsored by the Skokomish Indian Tribe with a grant from the Folk Arts Program of the National Endowment for the Arts. Exhibits at the Thomas Burke Memorial Museum in Seattle, the Washington State Historical Society in Tacoma, the State Capitol Museum in Olympia, the Oregon Historical Society in Portland, and the Whatcom Museum of History and Art in Bellingham used baskets from the Skokomish Tribal Collection to augment each museum's own collections.

A wealth of assistance was provided for the writing of the catalog. We wish to thank Martha George, Dickey Bradwell, Lawrence Webster, Bernard Adams, Ed Carriere and the staff of the Suquamish Tribe's Office of Cultural Programs for their help on Suquamish basketry; Harriet Shelton Dover for Snohomish, and Sally Snyder and Vi Hilbert for Skagit. We are also grateful to Del McBride (Nisqually), Donna Brownfield (Duwamish-Muckleshoot) and the late Lela Pulsifer (Sahewamish) for providing information on the Southern Puget Salish. Richard Cultee, Georgina Miller (recently deceased), Del Nordquist and Karen James offered their knowledge of Twana basketry. A special debt of gratitude is owed to the late Louisa Pulsifer of Skokomish, one of the last traditionally trained Twana weavers. A great deal of information on basketmaking was also learned from Fran and Bill James of Lummi.

For their long-standing help we particularly wish to thank Gregg Pavel, Research Assistant from the Skokomish Tribe, and the Twana Language and Culture Advisory Committee. The fruition of the catalog relied on the patience and talents of our editor Lane Morgan, designer Roselyn Pape and artist Margaret Davidson. All of the photography, except where otherwise noted, was done by Eduardo Calderón.

Puget Sound mussel gatherer with openweave utility baskets, circa 1898. From E.S. Curtis, The North American Indian, *vol. 9; courtesy of Historical Photography Collection, University of Washington Libraries.*

Introduction

In the myth period, before Indians appeared in the Puget Sound region, animals had many human qualities. Heron was the canoe builder, Beaver the woodsman, and Crow was the basketmaker. When the Transformer, or $duk^wibał$, came and changed the order of things into what they are today, Crow's baskets were turned into clam shells. The patterns on the shells today are what remain of the designs on her baskets. The original animals $duk^wibał$ changed became supernatural spirits that aided the Indians in various endeavors. It was Crow who provided help in basketmaking.

By its very nature basketry was closely integrated with the practical needs of a society based on hunting, fishing and gathering. Most food gathering and storage required a basket of one type or another. Size and construction technique were very much influenced by function. A basket for gathering and rinsing clams, for instance, had to be woven with open spaces to allow water and sand to filter out; likewise, one for storing dried clams would be of open weave to prevent infestation by mold. On the other hand, a basket used for boiling food had to be tightly made in order to hold water. Baskets served as suitcases, cupboards, lunch boxes, feast bowls, fish traps, hats and countless other items.

Basketry was by no means restricted to purely utilitarian purposes, however. Some baskets were made solely as beautiful objects to be admired and given away as gifts. Their prominence in the distribution of goods on ceremonial occasions and their preservation through generations of inheritance is an indication of their value.

Basketry was the major form of artistic expression practiced by women. Through training that began early in childhood, some women became specialists who were known for their technical skill and distinctive styles. A woman who wished to specialize in basketmaking sought the supernatural help of Crow to aid in her endeavor. She used specially prepared roots, grass and bark to create complex designs.

Early observers noted that the basketmakers of Puget Sound had mastered a great diversity of techniques — coiling, twining and plaiting — as well as distinctive decorative stitches. As a basketry region, Puget Sound is distinguished by a shared repertoire of techniques, materials and designs. Through ceremonial exchanges and intermarriage, techniques and designs were disseminated among the many village groups while certain individual and regional patterns remained distinct.

The Puget Sound region was in precontact times, as it is today, a comparatively heavily populated area. (When the first baskets were collected by explorers in 1841, the Indian population of Puget Sound, already greatly reduced by white man's diseases, was around 6,000 to 10,000.) It is characterized by seemingly innumerable inlets separated by narrow fingers of land and a scattering of islands. Ease of passage along the extensive waterways, combined with a large number of available food sources, made for an extremely hospitable environment. The inhabitants were Coast Salish peoples and as such related in language and culture to groups from British Columbia to the northern Oregon coast. Of the sixteen Coast Salish languages, the two found on Puget Sound were linguistically closer to each other than to any of the rest. This, combined with a common habitat and very similar cultures, provided the Sound residents with a strong bond.

The westernmost inlet, hook-shaped Hood Canal, was the home of the Twana, speakers of *tuwaduqucid*. The Puget Salish, who spoke *dx^wləsucid*, extended over the vast remainder of the Sound area. Both the Twana and Puget Salish consisted of a number of subgroups (now termed "tribes") made up of one or more villages speaking a common dialect. A village was composed of one or more households unified by strong kinship ties.

In the mid-1800s the nine Twana subgroups (Skokomish, Hoodsport, Duhlelap, Quilcene, Vance Creek, Tahuya, Dabob, Dosewallips and Duckabush) were moved onto a single reservation and became known as the Skokomish Tribe. Twana weavers elaborated the fancy soft twined basket (*t'qayas*) to a position of prominence. The *t'qayas*, with animal designs at the rim, became the hallmark of Twana basketry.

The Puget Salish maintained a strong tradition of coiled basketry, with some variation among the different groups. Linguistically the Puget Salish were divided into northern and southern sets of dialects. The Northern Puget Salish were comprised of the Skagit (of the Skagit watershed and offshore islands) and the Snohomish (along the Snohomish River

and offshore islands). The Southern Puget Salish were the Snoqualmie and Skykomish (these closely related groups were along the rivers of the same names), the Suquamish (on the eastern half of the Kitsap Peninsula and on Bainbridge Island), the Duwamish (along the rivers and creeks which form the Duwamish River, on Elliott and Shilshole bays, Lake Sammamish and Lake Washington), the Puyallup (in the Puyallup River system, on offshore islands and at the head of inlets west of the river mouth), the Nisqually (in the Nisqually River area), the Steilacoom (near the site of the modern-day town of that name and on Clover and Segwalichew Creeks), and the Sahewammish (at the mouth of McAllister Creek and the Nisqually River, and on the inlets at the southern end of the Sound).

Archaeological evidence of Salish basketry is relatively scarce due to the perishable nature of the materials, but surviving fragments demonstrate the antiquity of the art. The earliest documented museum pieces show the technical skill and mastery of design that marks a well-developed tradition. With the arrival of the military, traders, missionaries and settlers in the mid-nineteenth century, trade items began to replace some of the native made containers. Iron pots, enamelware, gunny sacks and oil tins came into household use. Baskets were still made for gathering, as gifts and for ceremonies, however, and an increasing demand for baskets by white collectors ensured the continuing manufacture of artistic forms. The influence of commercial sales was reflected in changes of size and materials, but the basic nature of traditional basketry remained much the same. It is this tradition, reaching back many generations, that is presented in *Crow's Shells*. A few individuals continue to work in this tradition today, and a growing appreciation for local native arts should ensure its persistence into the future.

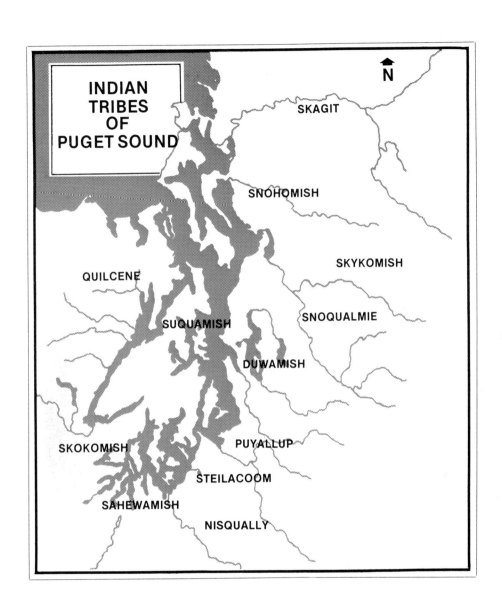

INDIAN
TRIBES
OF
PUGET SOUND

N

SKAGIT

SNOHOMISH

SKYKOMISH

QUILCENE

SNOQUALMIE

SUQUAMISH

DUWAMISH

PUYALLUP

SKOKOMISH

STEILACOOM

SAHEWAMISH

NISQUALLY

Two young girls with their mother in the White River hopfields, 1905. Traditional utilitarian baskets were used for harvesting this introduced commercial crop. Photograph by Asahel Curtis; courtesy of Historical Photography Collection, University of Washington Libraries.

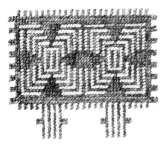

The Basketmakers

For the most part, the making of baskets was considered a woman's activity. A few men did learn to weave, especially if they were confined to the house because of illness or other disability. That the art was closely associated with the female sex is seen in the upriver Skagit custom of placing basketry materials under the sleeping platform of prospective parents if a girl was desired, while a bow and arrow was used to predestine a boy. (Collins 1974:216)

From infancy the children of Puget Sound societies grew up with basketry. Mothers and other female relatives kept young children with them as they performed the tasks of gathering shellfish, digging roots, cooking and picking berries, all of which required baskets. The mother of an infant kept her baby in a cradleboard nearby as she worked on making a basket.

Exceptional baskets played roles in stories told to children for entertainment and instruction. A Twana story about a girl who married an elk relates how "at bedtime she was given a large basket to sleep in, and as soon as she was inside they quickly laced the opening shut." (Curtis 1913:166) In a Nisqually story, as the girl who married a ghost arrived at the land of the dead "she found a diminutive old woman whose back was turned toward her as she sat weaving baskets from hair." The weaver was Screech Owl, "as much a person of the spirit land as of the earth." (Curtis 1913:132) A common theme on Puget Sound was for a child-stealing ogress to carry children away and eat them. In the Twana story "she had a live snake basket, woven of snakes, to carry children in" (Elmendorf 1960:35) while a Southern Puget Salish version tells how when "she was killed and transformed, the basket was transformed also, and is still to be seen on her back," as she was changed into Snail. (Waterman 1973:12-13)

Children imitated adult activities in their play. Boys joined in games of mock fishing, spearing and archery. Girls engaged in mock child care, followed later by playing house with toddlers in their charge, and elementary basketmaking. At about age six girls, and some boys as well, began to learn basic stitches by observing their mothers and other female relatives. First learned was the basket start, the flat piece which forms the bottom of a finished basket. As part of their play, young Skagit girls fashioned miniature baskets from materials they collected and prepared themselves. (S. Snyder 1964:259)

Both boys and girls assisted in the laborious tasks of gathering basketry materials. Cedar bark had to be stripped and split, cattails had to be cut and cleaned, and cedar roots of the proper size and shape had to be located and brought home. There was much to learn about when and where to seek materials and how to select and treat them.

Some girls chose to specialize in activities other

Twana weaver Phoebe Charley and her granddaughter Irene DanTeo on the Skokomish Reservation, circa 1905. Her baskets displayed here show her preference for horizontal designs and groups of three. Photograph courtesy of Del Nordquist.

than basketry, becoming root diggers, doctors, mat makers or blanket weavers. A girl who showed interest in learning the fine points of basketry apprenticed herself to an older relative or another respected basketmaker who made the type of basket she wished to learn. She performed household chores in exchange for instruction in complex stitches and specific designs.

Apprenticeship ended with the onset of the girl's first menstruation, or t'aq'^{w}ičad (Twana, refers to the breaking or snapping of a cord in the girl's back, which causes the bleeding). At the first sign of menstrual flow, a girl was removed to a menstrual hut located some distance from the village. Each girl had her own individual shelter, made of mats or branches, in which she remained day and night except when bathing. The period of seclusion ranged from one to eight months, depending on local custom.

Contact with a girl during her t'aq'^{w}ičad, and to a lesser extent all subsequent periods, brought dire consequences. It could drive off another's guardian spirit, magically weaken tools and weapons, spoil hunting and fishing, or even cause physical illness. The menstruating girl was supervised by an older female, usually a relative; a woman past menopause was preferred because she was least affected by the girl's state. The attendant assisted her in bathing, brought food and water, and gave her tasks to perform along with any necessary instruction.

Basketmaking was the usual task undertaken at this time and in many ways was linked symbolically with the change of the girl into a young woman. Most Puyallup, Steilacoom, Nisqually and Sahewammish girls did not make a complete basket on their own until their first menstruation. (Smith 1940:196) A Nisqually girl would make the bottom of a basket and a few coils of the side on the first day; on the second she began anew and worked nearer the finish. Each day she started a new basket until on her final day of seclusion she completed an entire basket. (Smith 1940:196) A Twana girl might weave a basket and then unravel it, subsequently

reusing the materials. (Elmendorf 1960:442) An upriver Skagit girl was expected to make four miniature baskets, measuring from three to four inches in diameter at the rim. Upon completion of each, she spit into it until it was filled with her saliva and discarded it. (S. Snyder 1964:262; Collins 1974:227) The products made by a Twana or Southern Puget Salish girl at this time were presented to older people, never kept.

It was through the tasks she was given and the habits she was taught during her seclusion that the young woman's character was to develop. An emphasis was placed on the importance of individual accomplishment, including the starting and completion of projects. She was to move quietly, talk little and sleep as few hours as possible. Failure to adhere to these taboos would leave her awkward, talkative and sleepy. If she failed to complete tasks once started, she would grow up lazy and never complete her work.

These instructions, expected to be carried out throughout the girl's adult life, also had implications for basketry. It was impressed upon a young Snohomish woman that basketmaking was a serious practice. If she giggled her stitches would be uneven. If she set her work aside and left it for later the sidewalls of the basket would contain bulges. If she did not concentrate her technique would be inconsistent.

The elaborate precautions of the t'aq'^{w}ičad were not repeated during a woman's later periods, and isolation lasted only as long as the menstrual flow. A woman spent this time in quiet seclusion, concentrating on basketmaking or other work. There were no restrictions placed on the products of her labor; what she made could be used by anyone.

The t'aq'^{w}ičad also marked the availability of a young woman for marriage. Intermarriage among Puget Sound groups was undoubtedly a factor in the transfer and exchange of basketry designs and techniques. Nearly all marriages were outside the village community (where the inhabitants were for the most part relatives) and the preferred arrangement was outside the group of closely related villages (or tribe). For example, the Southern Puget Salish married at least as far north as the Skagit and south to the Cowlitz, sometimes going east across the Cascade Mountains into Sahaptin-speaking areas. Usually the wife moved to her husband's home village.

In cases where her husband moved to her village or she married into a nearby village with a similar basketry tradition, a woman was able to continue using the knowledge and skills of basketmaking which she had acquired as a girl. Indeed, in the late nineteenth century the most famous basketmakers on the Skokomish Reservation were Twana women who had married Twana men.

When a woman married into a village which was not closely related to the village of her youth she might continue making the types of baskets she already knew how to make, she might adopt new styles from the women in her husband's community, or she might combine the basketry traditions of the two villages. A Hoodsport Twana woman named Big Anne, who lived at Bay Center on the Washington coast, continued to weave in the style of her home village. In addition she learned to make coastal style baskets. A Puyallup woman named Mattie Pulsifer was married to a Quilcene Twana on the Skokomish Reservation and continued to make Puyallup-style coiled baskets. By contrast, Celia

Satsop or Big Anne wove predominantly Twana soft twined baskets but also adopted styles from coastal peoples. In this 1906 postcard she is shown with soft twined baskets including one with a patriotic stars-and-stripes design as well as coiled and plaited works in the foreground. In the photograph on the facing page, the basket in the center foreground is made of spruce roots and has a vertical design similar to many Quinault baskets. (See Plate 34.) Postcard courtesy of Historical Photography Collection, University of Washington Libraries; photograph courtesy of John Gogol.

Anne Campbell, an Okanogan from eastern Washington who married an upriver Skagit, did not learn to make baskets until after her marriage and then adopted the techniques and designs of Skagit coiled basketry.

Women became known for making particular types of baskets. Those living at the same location might select basket types to complement one another, as was the case with three Suquamish sisters living near Agate Pass on the Kitsap Peninsula. Susie George made clam baskets and Mary Edgebert fish baskets. While Mary made some coiled baskets, it was Louisa Peter who was known for her elaborate coiled works.

Although many women made their own utilitarian baskets only a talented few were the specialists, q'ul'alči ("skilled basketmaker," Twana), who were absorbed in the aesthetic elaboration of decorated types, thereby gaining prestige and recognition. Some extended families excused these women from communal chores such as berry picking and clam drying in order to concentrate on basketry.

A young woman desiring superior talent in creating basketry designs sought to acquire a spirit power, as men did for skills such as sea mammal hunting and canoe building. After ritual fasting and bathing she went into the forest on a vision quest. The Skagit spirit c'ayq appeared to the woman from the east. He was a little bent-over man who had a house and a servant. He provided women who received his power with basketry designs. (Collins 1974:153; Haeberlin and Gunther 1930:71) The Southern Puget Salish associated basketmaking power with Crow, who had been an expert basketmaker. When the great transformation came, changing the world of the myth period to its present state, her baskets were turned into clam shells, their designs becoming the patterns of the shells.

In developing her individual style, a q'ul'alči was influenced by other basketmakers in her village, as well as her earlier training. From these sources she chose design elements which appealed to her, working them into patterns which became identified with her. Some designs did exist in the public domain

and could be used by all, but even those were often altered to fit individual expression. With basket-makers working in close proximity and serving as models, popular designs and manners of addressing the basket in terms of design fields, bottom starts and top finishing developed to form regional styles.

After becoming an accomplished basketmaker, a woman still recited the names of those whose works had provided inspiration. Basketmakers tended not to collect their own works but exchanged them with others, so any design which had become part of a master's repertoire had to be memorized.

It was through the potlatch, the most important social and ceremonial gathering among the people of Puget Sound, that many basketmakers gained widespread recognition. Large intertribal potlatches involved thousands of people representing over a dozen tribes and lasted as long as two weeks. The first days were consumed in formal arrivals, war dances by guest communities, religious ceremonies and feasting. These festivities were accompanied by contests and gambling. The final climactic event was the distribution of gifts to guests in order that the hosts might demonstrate their wealth; the greater the amount distributed, the higher their prestige. Each person receiving gifts was under an obligation to reciprocate by giving back a gift of equal or greater value in the future.

Potlatching stimulated the manufacture of goods since vast numbers of certain items were accumulated for years prior to the "giveaway." Sponsoring couples, with aid of relatives, worked hard to produce and acquire suitable gifts. Spouses were responsible for items they would give away to guests of their own sex; baskets fell exclusively under the category of female goods. Basketmakers enjoyed considerable prestige for the products of their labor, which were showcased in the giveaway.

Many women made their own utilitarian baskets. This weaver on the Skokomish Reservation in 1905 is seen with twilled cedar bark and cross-warp cedar root baskets. Photograph by Asahel Curtis; courtesy of Washington State Historical Society.

The principal time for making baskets was in the winter season, when families returned to their permanent residences after months of travel. The hard work of food gathering and preservation was over, and basketry materials had been obtained and prepared. As spring neared the pace increased: "When the Bumblebee flies into a house and buzzes near the women, he is asking them to make baskets quickly because the berries will ripen soon." (Jerry Kanim in Turner 1976:17) Weather permitting, construction was done outdoors; otherwise a woman positioned herself on the house floor near the fire, which provided both warmth and light. Seated on a mat, she kept the necessary materials and tools arranged conveniently about her. The bark, roots and grasses had to be dampened to keep them flexible while she worked. The singing of a power song sometimes accompanied the making of a basket. Like other power songs, it was associated with a special power and the lyrics had no meaning for others who heard it.

Older basketmakers, with eyes and hands not as strong as they had been, tended to change the types of baskets they made. Some makers of hard baskets, which required strength for splitting and sewing the roots, might shift to soft twining. Specialists in twining tended to use cattails, which are less difficult to manipulate and easily obtained. Designs were usually simplified, although they still retained a recognizable style. Older women often used basket starts made by children and in this way were able to direct their energy to the important work of making the designs on the sidewalls of baskets. After death, most of a woman's property was burned or placed with her body. Decorated baskets and basketry tools were instead passed on to female relatives.

A Suquamish weaver, Tennessee Napoleon George, seated in front of her home in Port Blakely around the turn of the century. Baskets include plaited and openweave bags from cattail, beargrass and cedar bark in addition to a cross-warp utility basket. A bundle of beargrass lies in the foreground. Photograph courtesy of Suquamish Tribal Archives.

Katie Weallup, a weaver on the Tulalip Reservation, soaking cedar roots in front of her temporary shelter during the fishing season of 1905. Photograph by Norman Edson; courtesy of Historical Photography Collection, University of Washington Libraries.

Materials and Dyes

The preliminary steps in the making of any basket involved the gathering and preparation of materials. These tasks — location and selection of roots, barks and grasses, cutting, drying and other treatments — consumed at least as much time as the actual weaving. Baskets with artistic designs required supplementary materials as well as extra preparation and construction time. Children were trained to assist in gathering activities, and men participated by watching for exposed cedar roots while fishing.

As with food plants, there were certain seasons and locations for collecting each of the plant parts used in basketmaking. Women typically returned to the same sites year after year. Conditions such as weather, elevation and amount of sunlight influenced the time when a particular plant was ready. Often changes in nearby food plants were linked to the readiness of basketry materials. For example, it was said that when red elderberries were ripe it was time to gather sweetgrass. Timing was all important. If gathered too early, beargrass would be too small

Cattails laid out flat to dry on the porch of an elderly Puget Sound couple's home. Photograph by Anders Wilse; courtesy of Historical Photography Collection, University of Washington Libraries.

and would shrivel up when dried; if gotten too late it would be brittle.

Knowledge of gathering times and locations was shared by basketmakers within a family and passed on to the next generation. Locally coined place names aided basketmakers in remembering and discussing sites. The sole source of spruce roots within a twenty-mile stretch of shoreline was reflected in "Spruce Tree Creek," and a prime location for mud used in dyeing was termed "Alot-of-Sticky-Mud."

Basketry materials were never used in their raw state but had to be sorted, cleaned, dried, often split, and prepared in other ways. Some of this work was done while the bark, root or grass was being collected. The exact method of processing varied some from weaver to weaver, but there were definite steps that had to be followed for each material. The materials were then stored and used so as to extend through the entire winter season.

MATERIALS

Beargrass (*Xerophyllum tenax*)

This member of the lily family has also been called pine lily, squawgrass, mountain grass, deergrass, elkgrass, turkeybeard, American grass and basket grass. On Puget Sound, however, it was known by only two names: xǝlalsǝd (Twana, referring to its use in designs) and č'ǝtulbix^w (Puget Salish, referring to the plume at the end of the stalk). It ranges from near sea level in the Hood Canal area to over 7,000 feet in both the Cascade and Olympic mountains.

Beargrass was used as a decorative material on both utilitarian and fancy baskets. Its durability and strength made it particularly appealing. The

Beargrass in bloom has a showy plume of small white flowers. The stiff grass-like leaves are used to decorate many types of baskets. Photograph by Albert H. Barnes; courtesy of Historical Photography Collection, University of Washington Libraries.

leaves, which have a sheen, were bleached white in the sun, or dyed yellow with bark from the Oregon grape plant or black with a special mud. Purple, blue, orange and other hues were added with the introduction of commercial dyes.

Beargrass leaves were gathered during the summer when they were soft, succulent, long and resilient. The center strands were bunched together, wound once around the hand and jerked upward. The narrow strands were then separated from the wide ones and bunches of sorted grass were braided at one end. These were placed outside to dry and bleach for about two weeks, being taken inside at night. After drying the grass was stored in a dry place. Before it could be used in weaving, the ridge or "backbone" that runs down the center of each strand had to be removed. Then the strands were trimmed to an even width using special wooden trimmers.

Because of its fine decorative qualities, beargrass was both a welcome gift and a valuable trade article in pre-contact times. Not having beargrass in their valley, the upriver Skagit traded for it with the Snoqualmie and adjacent eastern Washington groups. (Collins 1974:68) The Twana, who had easy access to it, traded it to the Upper Chehalis and probably the Suquamish, and in more recent times (the early 1900s) to the Makah.

Cattail (*Typha latifolia*)

The cattail grows in standing, shallow fresh water throughout the Puget Sound region. The stalks without catkins, termed females in Puget Sound languages although they are botanically the males, have softer cores and less rounded leaves. These were the ones used for making soft baskets of various types and mats.

Puget Sound women gathering cattails. From E.S. Curtis, The North American Indian, *vol. 9; courtesy of Historical Photography Collection, University of Washington Libraries.*

Cattails were gathered from early July to early August before they became dry. Those growing in shade could be obtained later and those found near salt water were felt to be the strongest. The leaves were cut near the base and allowed to drain for a few days. They were then gutted by running the thumb down the center of the leaf and separating the outside jacket. Gutting prevented molding during the drying process which took several weeks. The soft outer edge was used in weaving baskets.

Cattails were often the material chosen for young Twana girls to practice with for their first baskets. And, in a Puget Sound woman's elder years, she might again turn from constructing watertight baskets from roots, a process requiring great finger strength, to working with cattails because they are soft and pliable.

Western Red Cedar (*Thuja plicata*)

To the innumerable uses of western red cedar in the making of houses, canoes, boxes, clothing and other items must be added its extensive utilization in basketry. In the Puget Sound area, the roots and bark were used in the manufacture of artistically decorated baskets.

Cedar roots were used primarily in coiled and openweave baskets. Long roots without much branching were the ideal. Those growing along rotten logs were apt to have the desired qualities and could be removed by breaking apart the decaying wood. Roots were also gathered along river and stream banks where they were exposed by erosion or dug from underground with a hardwood digging stick, a more arduous process. To protect the tree only a few pieces of root were taken at any one time.

Once the roots had been collected, they were peeled and split. A knife was used to start the split and then one portion was held in the teeth while the other was pulled away in a downward motion. The inside portions of the root were used for the foundation of the coiled basket, and the outside pieces became the sewing strands. Cedar roots are tough and durable, dense enough to make a completely watertight container when stitched closely together.

Wooden trimmers set with metal blades replaced mussel shell knives for the purpose of cutting strips of beargrass or cedar bark. Three different widths of beargrass were cut, each corresponding to a different fineness of weave. Photograph by Eduardo Calderón, (WSHS loan)

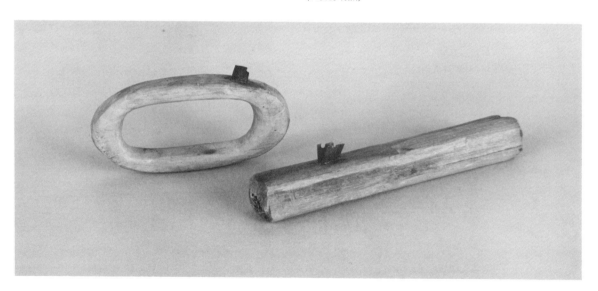

The inner bark of cedar had many uses in traditional culture, for clothing, towels, diapers and ceremonial paraphernalia as well as baskets. When it was pounded and shredded, cedar bark became very soft. For use in baskets it was split into different thicknesses and widths but was not shredded.

Cedar bark was stripped from the trees while the sap was still running, usually between May and July before the bark got too sticky and difficult to pull off. Small trees about a foot in diameter were preferred; those with low branches were avoided. Only one or two strips were taken from each tree. Gatherers made a horizontal cut about two or three feet above the ground and then pulled straight up on the bark to get a long, even strip. Strips were at least four or five inches wide and as long as twenty feet. Batches of the collected strips were folded into bundles and taken home to be peeled. Only the inner bark was used in weaving, and it had to be separated from the shaggy outer layer while it was still moist.

A light, creamy color when fresh, inner bark turns reddish gold on exposure to light and eventually may become dark brown with use. A certain kind of mud was used to dye the bark black, and a paste made of alder bark turned it red. Various widths and thicknesses were obtained by splitting and trimming with the same wooden tool used for beargrass.

Cedar bark was frequently used for plaited bags, for the bottoms and warps of twined baskets, and occasionally as the weft in openweave baskets. It is also found as the decorative overlay material on soft twined baskets, and sometimes as imbrication on coiled baskets.

Horsetail, Scouring Rush (*Equisitum* sp.)

The bark from the roots of certain species of horsetail and scouring rush were used for imbrication on coiled baskets. The bark was collected in short pieces after digging up the roots that extend deep underground. Colors range from coal black to purplish black and the surface has a characteristic wrinkled appearance when it dries.

Wild Cherry (*Prunus emarginata*)

Another material frequently found as imbrication on coiled baskets is the bark of the wild cherry tree. The bark grows in a distinctive circular fashion around the trunk, making it possible to peel it off in a spiral. The Twana name for the tree refers to this characteristic: *yəliałpi* "turns around the trunk."

The outer bark was removed by making an incision about one-half to one inch wide and then peeling it around and around the trunk or limb. Although the bark is a dull color in its natural state, when scraped and rubbed it becomes glossy and red. Wild cherry bark is a more durable material than horsetail roots and wears better on a basket.

Maidenhair Fern (*Adiantum pedatum*)

The purplish black stem of the maidenhair fern was occasionally employed for decoration. It is too narrow to be used for imbrication but can be inserted as an overlay strand on twined baskets.

The late Emily Miller, Skokomish weaver, removing cedar bark from a tree. Photograph by Del Nordquist; courtesy of the photographer.

23

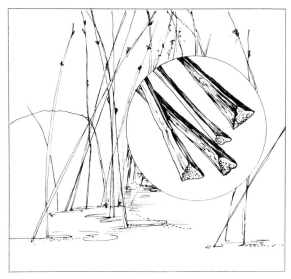

Sweetgrass plants with detail of stem.

Sweetgrass (*Scirpus Americanus* Pers.)

Like other sedges, sweetgrass has a distinctive three-cornered stem. It grows in tidal flats where salt water reaches over the shore. Formerly it could be found in pockets around Puget Sound, but today the prime locations for gathering are along the Pacific coast at Grays Harbor and Willapa Bay.

The gathering season was generally between July and early August. The earlier in the year, the shorter the grass; by late August it might get brittle and hard to pull. At low tide, the gatherer could reach the grass and pull it up by the roots. Long strands were highly desirable, but shorter ones could be used for making smaller baskets.

To prepare the grass for weaving, it was set out to dry for three to four days until it was bleached, so that all the green color was gone. Then it was cleaned and the outer jackets removed by running a mussel shell, or deer's leg bone down each strand with the thumb on the underside. This process also took out any excess moisture and flattened and softened the grass for weaving. Further drying took

place indoors in a dry spot or outdoors if the weather was sunny. The thick grass was then split to an even width with a fingernail.

Sweetgrass was seldom dyed for basketmaking but used in its natural straw-yellow color. It is found as both warp and weft on twined baskets.

DYES

Oregon Grape (low bush *Berberis nervosa*; high bush *Berberis aquifolium*)

Beargrass was dyed yellow with a dye made from the bark of the Oregon grape. Although the root bark of the low bush species was more widely used, in areas where it was available bark from the limbs of the high bush variety were substituted or mixed in. Obtaining high bush bark was less work as it didn't require digging, washing and cleaning. High bush dye was also more intense so less bark was needed.

The bark was gathered in the summer when it was easier to remove. To make the dye, the bark was bruised and then boiled in water. The beargrass was then either put into the boiling dye for fifteen to thirty minutes or left to stand in a cooled dyebath for two to seven days. In both cases the length of time in the dye determined the darkness of the yellow.

Red Alder (*Alnus rubra*)

The bark of this familiar deciduous tree was used to make a red dye which was applied to cedar bark. The dye had to be applied to the bark while the cedar was still fresh, presumably because of the interaction of the dye with the sap, so an alder with thin bark was selected at the same time the cedar bark was being gathered. Hunks of alder bark were removed with a knife. The dead outer bark and the inner cambium layer were peeled away and the remaining middle layer was smashed to a paste and applied directly onto the cedar bark. Traditionally, the paste was made by chewing the bark and spitting the juice onto the cedar. In more recent times it was pounded and mixed with a few drops of water.

The dye was spread onto the bark in the hot sun so that it would dry quickly and not turn too dark. Once the dye had taken, the excess was rubbed off and the cedar bark folded up and stored.

Black Mud

A smooth-textured, dark grey-blue mud was used as a black dye for cedar bark and beargrass. It was found in deposits at certain places along rivers and creeks in brackish water.

In order to dye properly, cedar bark had to be at least one year old. The bark was submerged in the mud and left overnight after mud had been rubbed on its inner side. The length of time required to dye varied but if left in the mud for more than two weeks the bark might begin to rot. After removing the bark from the mud it was rinsed, allowed to dry and then folded while it was still flexible.

Western Hemlock (*Tsuga heterophylla*)

The bark of this evergreen tree was used by some Puget Sound groups to dye fish nets a muddy brown color, so that they blended in with the water. The dye was also found marginally in basketry. The bark was pounded and placed in water, and the material soaked in that mixture.

Lichens

Certain type of lichens were infrequently employed for making dyes. The Twana used one type which yielded a green color resembling a leaf in spring.

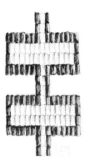

Coiled Baskets

3

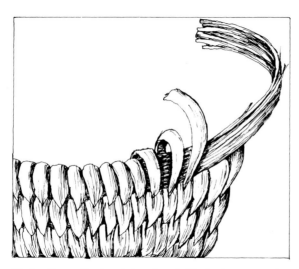

The bundle or splint foundation of a coiled basket is sewn together with lengths of split cedar root.

The technique of coiling allowed for the construction of watertight baskets for a variety of purposes, including cooking (with heated stones boiling water within the basket); serving soups and stews; picking, transporting and storing berries (the solid structure protected and held the juicy fruit); and transporting water. When wet the roots from which the baskets were made swelled to make them completely watertight. In addition to utilitarian functions, coiled works were prime recipients of artistic decoration. Fancy ones were presented as gifts and passed on from one generation to the next. Puget Sound coiled baskets are among the most skillfully constructed in the world.

TECHNIQUE

The Puget Sound coiled basket was made of split peeled roots. The two outer sections, which are smoother, became the sewing strands and the inner pieces, which are more brittle and rough, formed the foundation. The sewing material was scraped thin and flat prior to use. Primarily cedar roots were utilized but some makers used spruce instead.

The foundation, or coil, was composed of a bundle of root sections of varying size and length, packed closely together. Generally, the larger the basket, the thicker the coil. The coil was wound around to form the base and then extended for the sidewalls.

The types of coiled bottoms found on Puget Sound baskets, in order of occurrence, were meander, spiral, parallel and slat. The meander, the most common, is an oval start which begins with an element placed lengthwise and following coils wound around it. The spiral is a perfectly round coil. The parallel start has the bundles doubled in accordian-like fashion to form a rectangle or oval. The rare slat method, found occasionally on Puget Sound baskets, has one or more flat pieces of cedar in the center, covered with stitches which attach it to the coils which surround it.

The infrequent use of cedar slat coils for sidewalls by the upriver Skagit was a result of influence by neighbors to the north in British Columbia where it was a common practice. The slat coils are wider and flatter than their bundle coil counterparts. Since slat coils do not swell when wet, they cannot be used in constructing a watertight container.

In the process of coiling, the foundation is held together with stitches. Puget Sound coiling contains four types of stitches based on two variables. Sewing strands of a higher coil may connect to the immediately lower coil either by piercing its foundation or by interlocking with its sewing stitches. As a stitch is made, it can split the stitch immediately below it (called bifurcation) or be inserted between two stitches. Interlocking with bifurcation is the most common process, sometimes forming a decorative surface. The number of stitches per inch ranges from four to twelve, the latter being an extremely fine example. An average basket combines five coils and seven stitches per inch.

After soaking the roots to make them flexible, the Puget Sound basketmaker began her coiled basket by sewing the initial portion of the foundation. She then fashioned the coil and stitched it together as she went. Right-handed women worked in a clock-

The Twana basket in the center has a clockwise meander base, while the two Puget Salish examples have spiral starts. (Burke 1-700, 1-11202, 1-805)

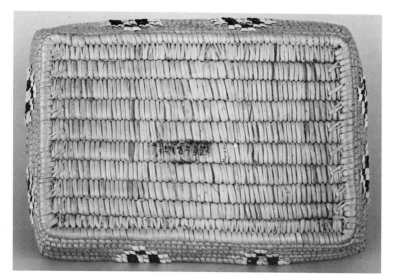

wise direction, pulling a long strand through holes made in the foundation with an awl. The strands were pushed down through a hole in the preceding coil, wrapped back around the new row and put through the neighboring hole.

The sewing material was rubbed with water to keep it pliable. When it ran down to its last two-and-a-half to three inches a new strand was inserted by running it through the last hole entered by the old piece. The end of the latter was folded into the foundation and the new sewing element pulled tight so that the stump of the old was barely visible on the outer surface of the basket. New foundation elements were added in the center of strands already in use.

The sewing was done from the outside to the inside of the basket with the sewing material kept at right angles to the coil. The sides were sloped outward by gradually increasing the circumference of each coil. Generally, the bottom and mouth were round or oval and the sides flared part of the way up.

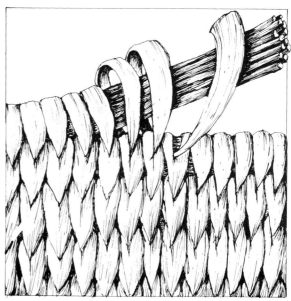

Bifurcation of stitches.

TOP—Duwamish basket with slat bottom. (Burke 1-10792)
BOTTOM—A Puget Sound basket with parallel coil base. (Burke 1-1969)

As she worked, the basketmaker strove to keep the basket well formed. The base was supposed to be flat and the sidewalls smooth and even. Strands were sewn tightly together in order to conceal the foundation underneath and to produce a rigid, firm basket. The foundation itself was to be kept at an even thickness, even where adding was done. When each coil was finished, the woman turned the basket upside down to judge the evenness of the coils.

Final coils range from finely tapered to abrupt endings. The rims of Puget Sound baskets were of three types: plain, braided and looped. A plain rim is simply the final coil wrapped with its sewing stitches. A braided rim, by far the most common

Decorative loops at the rim. (Burke 2.5-562)

BELOW — The hands of Julia Siddle, Duwamish of the Muckleshoot Reservation, inserting sewing strand around a coil. Photograph by Erna Gunther; courtesy of Historical Photography Collection, University of Washington Libraries.

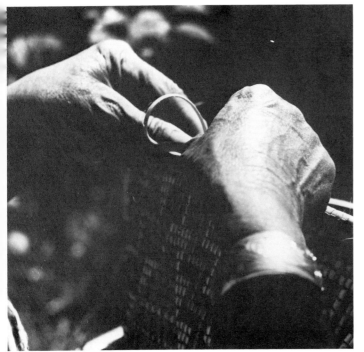

Detail of beading on a Suquamish cooking basket. (Burke 8664)

29

A tumpline could be worn across the chest or around the forehead for carrying loads. This Puget Sound woman is shown on the beach, perhaps at West Seattle. Photograph by Anders Wilse; courtesy of Historical Photography Collection, University of Washington Libraries.

Imbrication.

type, was constructed by sewing and twisting an additional strand over the final coil in a braid-like fashion. Some fancy baskets were ornamented with loops placed in rows on top of the last row of coiling. These added loops may be either flat or steep in angle; they can be in the form of a single row of scallop-like loops, a double set of interlocking loops, or an elaborate stacked series of loops. Another decorative detail is an additional twisted strand of beargrass twined in just below the braided rim.

The major decorative technique used on Puget Sound coiled baskets was imbrication, an overlapping of added materials of contrasting color and texture. Material for imbrication was inserted as the sewing was being done. A strip was laid down on the foundation, caught with a stitch and then doubled back, with the next stitch catching the fold. Then it was drawn over the second stitch, thereby concealing the sewing on the outside of the basket.

The design capabilities of this technique allowed basketmakers to create a number of distinctive patterns. The materials used on Puget Sound baskets were beargrass for white and yellow, wild cherry bark for red, and horsetail or dyed cedar bark for black. The imbrication technique itself was confined to the geographic area stretching between the lower third of British Columbia to the Washington-Oregon border.

Beading was done in a similar manner. A strand of beargrass was placed on the coil, and without any folding was passed under and over a certain number of stitches. As it passed over the sewing material it became visible as a design on the outside. The beaded strips usually pass over only one or two stitches at a time. Beading can be either the sole decoration on a basket or it can be combined with imbrication, where it breaks up an otherwise plain background. It is more commonly found on basket bottoms than imbrication.

A coiled basket was made in a size and shape to fit its intended use. Cooking baskets were apt to be large, 10 to 16 inches in height with very rounded flared sides which are slightly inturned at the top surrounding an oval mouth. An extremely large cooking basket could hold up to eight gallons. (Eells ms.)

Other large coiled baskets were used for packing and storage of dry goods. These occur in a variety of forms, some taller and with straighter sides than the cooking baskets. Those made by the upriver Skagit in particular were very deep and straight-sided. Four pairs of holes were pierced near the rim of the completed basket using a deer bone awl. Loops made of buckskin or fiber string were attached through these perforations so that the contents could be tied inside when being carried or stored. They were positioned two to a side, occupying the long sides of oblong works. Each thong was passed through a pair of holes and tied on each internal end. The thongs themselves were then used to attach tumplines or for strapping on covers.

The tumpline, or k'a<del>l</del>i (Twana, "hangs from the head") was a woven band with long braids on either end. The wide center portion was placed over the forehead or across the chest with the braided lines reaching back to support the load. Occasionally for stability in taller packing baskets, lower thongs were also attached.

In picking berries the tumpline went across the picker's chest, with the loose ends tied around her waist, thus securing the basket in front of the picker, leaving her hands free. Often a smaller basket was

A Muckleshoot girl with two coiled baskets and traditional cedar bark clothing. The smaller basket was used for picking berries and the larger one for transporting them. Photograph courtesy of Suquamish Tribal Archives; original in Smithsonian Institution.

31

employed for this purpose and when it became full the berries were dumped into a larger basket to be transported home when filled. The baskets used in picking berries were from 6½ to 10 inches in height. They held an average of two quarts. (Eells ms.) Other baskets of very similar shape but smaller (from 2½ to 5½ inches tall) were typically used by children for picking berries. Many young girls were given miniature baskets as gifts and kept them throughout adult life.

Shallow bowl-shaped baskets were made like the pack baskets except that they were finished off while the sides were still short, ranging from 3½ to 6 inches in height with a mouth diameter between 8 and 11 inches. Bases are either round or oval, and the rims often have a decorative row of scalloplike loops around the top. In recent times they have served to hold sewing materials and jewelry.

"Nut-shaped" baskets of Puget Sound were most prevalent among the Nisqually but were made by others such as the Suquamish. These expand outward from the base and then retract to a narrow mouth. Shapes range from oval to round. Leather or fiber thongs near the rim were used to attach flat coiled lids. The Nisqually examples resemble neighboring Klickitat ones used for storage and water jars.

A basketmaker was able to highlight her skill by making either miniature or oversize baskets. In this virtuoso tradition, a Muckleshoot woman made a huge 3½-foot-tall coiled basket not designed for utility, but to show that such a project could be done. (Smith and Leadbetter 1949:113) In contrast to this oversized work, a totally imbricated basket only 1½ inches high was made by a Puyallup basketmaker. This miniature work, with 12 weft stitches per inch, has loopwork on the rim and a row of beading on the base. It was presented before

LEFT—Minnie Richards, born in 1884 and the daughter of Puyallup leader Tyee Dick Sinnaywah, displays items of wealth indicative of her status—an elaborately coiled basket, beaded bag and headband, and Pendleton blanket. Photograph by A.C. Carpenter; courtesy of Historical Photography Collection, University of Washington Libraries.

Catherine Mounts of Nisqually with her extensive collection of baskets, several of which were made by Nancy Parsons, Nisqually-Cowlitz. Photograph courtesy of Washington State Capitol Museum and the Mounts family.

1938 to a Snohomish dignitary at an intertribal gathering.

Specially made and highly decorated coiled baskets were distributed as gifts which accompanied marriages and potlatches. They were accumulated over long periods of time and exchanged in mint condition. Usually they were made without the thongs which were inserted into coiled baskets made for use. At feasts food was served in special, extremely large coiled baskets. After the meal baskets of fresh water were passed around for people to rinse their mouths. (Smith 1940:229)

While much of an individual's property was disposed of at the death of the owner, "coiled baskets and large canoes were regarded not as personal property but an inheritable, as property which had a longer life span than any single individual." (Smith 1940:203) When a woman died these baskets were inherited by close female relatives, such as her sisters or daughters. It was not unusual for a basket's owner to be able to trace the female line of ownership back as many as five generations.

A basket with "sword fern" design is used to hold wool being carded by Alice Gus and spun by Mary Moses of Tulalip in 1898. Photograph by Edward S. Curtis; courtesy of Historical Photography Collection, University of Washington Libraries.

The rim design area of a Suquamish basket, a geometric rim design. (Burke 1-1910)

DESIGNS

All Puget Sound tribes produced elaborately ornamented coiled baskets. It was in the application of designs that the basketmaker exhibited the height of her artistic skills. When placing a design on her basket, she could leave the background plain, showing the sewing strands, or imbricate the entire surface, or create a spotted white surface with the use of beading. After a color scheme was selected, the design was built up row by row as the basket was constructed, bottom to top. Some designs were placed uniformly around the basket while others were arranged on the four sides. To attain proper symmetry, the design had to be conceptually mated to the basket surface.

Although a weaver made use of a body of traditional designs, she was allowed some freedom in their rendition. Designs were passed down by female relatives, learned from trainers and borrowed from the works of other basketmakers. Weavers were not restricted to existing patterns, however. New designs came through spirit power dreams and artistic innovations.

Names were applied to the designs of coiled baskets. The general term for a design was *sx̌alulač*, "basket design." As a general rule, the name of the object represented was suffixed by *-ulač*, "basket," to form the name of the particular design. For example, *c'ayat*, "salmon gills," as a design was termed *c'ayatulač*. In some Indian communities designs survived longer than their names. Today only a very few people are able to name any coiled basketry designs. Among the Twana, where names of soft basket designs are still known, the terms for designs found only on hard baskets have disappeared.

In composing a design, a basketmaker either treated the entire surface of a basket as a single field or divided it into two separate horizontal fields. When there are two fields, the upper one is a narrow band that contains a row of simple geometric elements such as triangles or rectangles. In addition, Twana baskets sometimes contain zoomorphic designs in this area. This rim design area is often set apart from the main body of the basket by a change in background color. The main design field is the central visual focus of the basket. On this surface the basketmaker chose between four arrangements: horizontal, vertical, diagonal and all-over. Diagonal designs could slant in one direction only or create opposing lines.

35

MAIN DESIGNS

1. RECTANGULAR.

BOXES/STARFISH - The Puget Salish had two versions of what they termed "boxes," each based on rectangles placed in a vertical series, connected by one or two lines. The more common of the two is the unclosed version with either a single (found among the Skagit) or double (found among the Snohomish and Sahewamish) outline. These unclosed versions were both used by the Twana and termed "starfish." The closed version is akin to the Twana soft-basket "boxes" design but is not found on Twana coiled work but rather on Northern Puget Salish examples. The Thompson, Lillooet, Upper and Lower Chehalis and Quinault had designs similar to these patterns.

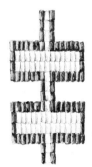

HOUSEFLY/STAR - This is a frequent design on Puget Salish baskets, either as a main or rim design. It is made up of four small squares with one corner of each touching and with a contrastingly colored square in the center. The Twana name "star" is the same as that used by the Quinault while the Puget Salish name of "fly" matches those of the Lillooet and Thompson.

DRAGONFLY - Found on a basket made by Sally Jackson who lived at the Puyallup village at Whollochet Bay, this design consists of horizontal bands placed inside a long column with an "I"-shaped figure at the bottom.

SWORD FERN - A Duwamish basketmaker from Renton who married a White River Duwamish used this design, a vertical white stripe separating two columns of black rectangles. This pattern depicts the shape of the fronds of the sword fern.

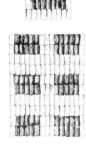

2. TRIANGULAR.

BUTTERFLY - Triangles are arranged in vertical rows with points down, usually touching each other. Baskets from the Skagit, Snohomish, Suquamish, Nisqually, Duwamish, Sauk-Suiattle and Twana have been observed with this design.

NOTCHED ROOF BEAM - small triangles with stepped sides run vertically with points down. Made by Mrs. Jimmy Moses, a Duwamish, the steps represent the notches that hold the sheeting poles of a house roof.

FISH NET - Intersecting diagonal lines form diamond-shaped spaces over the entire background of the basket. Found among the Twana, Skagit, Suquamish and Nisqually.

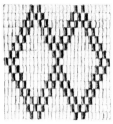

MOUNTAIN - Small triangles are placed inside wide zig-zag bands that are either stepped or straight-sided. This design is quite common throughout the Puget Salish and has several variations. Observed among Duwamish, Steilacoom, Sauk-Suiattle and Suquamish.

FLOUNDER - Vertically stacked diamonds are arranged in rows on Twana and Snohomish baskets, representing the flat fish of this shape at least among the former. This design, with the same name, is also found on Quinault baskets.

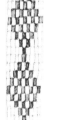

3. LINEAR.

SNAKE - A series of stepped lines slant diagonally across the basket, either up to the right or left. Often lines are of contrasting colors, such as black/white/black/white alternations. This design was used among the Snohomish, Puyallup, downriver Skagit, Suquamish and Twana.

SALMON GILLS - The pattern, widespread among the Skagit, Snohomish, Puyallup, Suquamish and Twana, usually is arranged in large vees that encircle the basket. Horizontal background stripes accompanying this design are made by Mrs. Dave Squally at Whollochet Bay to represent *salmon ribs*.

SPREAD OUT - A representation of a plant that spreads out as a fern does, this Southern Puget Salish design is found on Puyallup and Suquamish works.

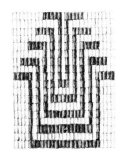

INTERSECTING - Made by Mary Sam at Suquamish, this design is like the *fish net* except that the lines are horizontal and vertical rather than diagonal.

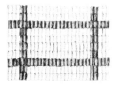

4. REALISTIC.

HUMANS - Southern Puget Salish baskets occasionally contain representations of human figures. Females are distinguished from males on a Nisqually basket by skirts and a smaller waist. On Nisqually and Puyallup examples both feet and hands are depicted. When fingers are shown they number three. On a Puyallup basket four men are standing in a row holding hands waist high. On a Nisqually work the figures are placed randomly in two rows, some with lowered hands some with raised hands.

DOGS - These appear on Twana coiled works much as they do on soft twined baskets, with four straight legs and a tail which points up from the rear leg and turns back toward the back of the head. They are found going either to the right or the left.

HELLDIVER - This type of grebe has a slightly different appearance on Twana coiled baskets than it does on their twined work: A coiled helldiver faces to the left with its two legs slanting down to the left.

Rim designs are not found on all decorated Puget Sound coiled baskets. Some rim designs such as "dog" and "fly/star" are the same as main designs, while others are found only on the rim. The names of these designs are less documented than those of the main design field. No Puget Salish names are known, and the only Twana names known are those which are also found on soft twined baskets.

SAMPLE RIM DESIGNS

SPIDER WEB - This Twana design is a zig-zag pattern in which the triangular shapes formed are not shaded.

TRIANGLE - The length of these ranges from a mere two coils wide (characteristic of the Suquamish) to four coils wide (made by Mrs. Jimmy Moses, a Duwamish).

CHAIN - Two types have been observed, one of two coils width (on Suquamish and Duwamish baskets) and another three coils wide (on Twana and Duwamish works).

4

Soft Twined Baskets

Twining is one of the most ancient forms of weaving, found almost universally among the cultures of the world. Archeological evidence shows twining to have been practiced by the Coast Salish for at least 3,000 years, based on baskets uncovered at a Musqueam Halkomelem site in southwestern British Columbia. By contrast, the oldest Salish coiling example, from a Swinomish site near La Conner, dates back only about 1,200 years. (Croes 1979:96) This would seem to indicate that coiling was a more recent technology than twining among the Coast Salish, but it should be noted that excavated sites in the region are most often temporary fishing camps, where utilitarian twined baskets were more likely to be discarded after use.

The nature of the elements woven in twining allows for production of either a stiff unbendable basket or a soft flexible one. Stiff twined baskets were made for trapping fish, gathering fish and shellfish, and other uses requiring a rigid container. These utilitarian baskets displayed minimal decoration, most frequently in the form of beargrass strips overlaid on warp elements. Soft twined baskets, however, received much artistic elaboration by some Puget Salish basketmakers.

Soft twined baskets served as storage containers for household goods such as clothing and blankets. They were either round and deep or flared with shorter sides. The deep variety could be folded shut and tied with string at the top. The usual location for storing goods of all kinds was on cedar plank shelves that lined the walls of the winter residence. The size and weight of an article determined the size, material and construction of the basket in which it was to be stored. Large soft baskets were appropriate for holding clothing while small ones were used for valuables such as dentalia shells.

TECHNIQUE

The technique of twining differs from coiling in that it is the horizontal element, or weft, that is actively engaged in weaving, while the vertical elements, or warps, remain passive. Several varieties of twining are found on Puget Sound baskets. The simplest form is plain twining, in which two wefts cross each other between warps. The weft on the inside is brought to the outside and the outside one is turned to the inside. A half twist is made around each warp strand. The weft rows of soft twined baskets are packed closely together to conceal the warps.

In the construction of a plain twined basket, the weaver began by making the center of the bottom. The exact method of starting varied considerably, even from individual to individual, but most represent variations on a basic theme. A number of warps were arranged like spokes of a wheel and

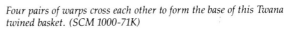
Four pairs of warps cross each other to form the base of this Twana twined basket. (SCM 1000-71K)

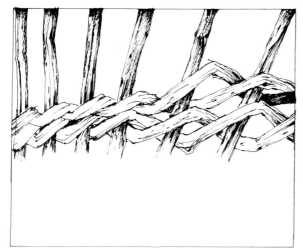
Plain twining.

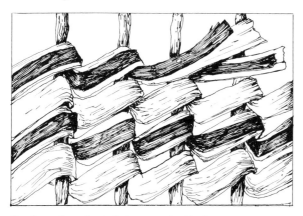
Overlay, a decorative technique on twined baskets.

An overlay of cedar bark and beargrass completely covers the cattail foundation of a Twana soft twined basket. (WSHS T138)

The inside of the rim of a Twana basket showing reverse color pattern created with full-twist overlay. (Burke 1-1190)

Wrapped twining.

twining proceeded around the warps from the center outward in radial fashion. Variations involved the number and arrangement of warps. In a simple start, four warp elements were arranged in pairs that cross at the center. In more complex forms, sixteen or more warps were grouped in pairs or fours and converged to create an intricate pattern.

When the weaver reached the point where she wanted to finish the bottom of her basket, she often made a row of twining using three strands instead

of two. This row appears as a raised braid-like stitch and serves as a transition between the bottom and the sides. To start the sides, she bent the warps sharply upward. The weaver kept the bottom of the basket turned toward her, rotating it continually as she worked. A right-handed person would hold the warps with her left hand and manipulate the weft strands with her right. The shape of the sides was maintained by controlling the tension of the weaving and by adding new warps. Keeping the tension as even as possible, the weaver caught each new warp in a twist and incorporated it with the original warp.

When viewed with the basket set upright, the stitches of a twined basket have a characteristic slant. They may slant down to the left or down to the right. This characteristic is called pitch. The direction of the pitch is determined by the way the weaver twists her wefts: when proceeding clockwise, if the outside weft is placed on the top, the pitch will be down to the left; if the inside weft twists over the outside, the pitch will be down to the right. When the weaving moves counterclockwise, the direction of the twist is reversed. The twined baskets of Puget Sound usually exhibit leftward pitch.

Three-strand twining was often used for the final rows at the top of the sidewalls. The rim of the basket was finished by turning the warp strands down on the inside and holding them in place with a row of twining. The warps were then cut off close to the body of the basket. Sometimes loops were added to the rim, originally for tying the basket closed and later for decoration. A finished basket was filled with damp sand, then smoothed and shaped with the hands. When the sand dried it was poured out and the basket held its shape.

The simplest form of decoration on a plain twined basket involved the substitution of colored strands in the weft. When colored elements replace both wefts a solid colored row is formed. When only one strand is inserted an every-other-stitch coloration, or beaded effect, is the result.

Another decorative technique used on Puget Sound plain twining was overlay, which involves

40

the use of extra strands laid on top of one or both structural wefts. The overlay strands contrast in color and texture with the structural materials. As the weft which is being covered is given a half twist around each warp, the overlay is given the same twist as well. When the overlay lies on top of only one structural weft the exterior wall shows the overlay every other stitch, providing a beaded effect. If both wefts are covered the contrasting overlay is continuous. By changing the material of the overlay, complex patterns of different colors can be created. The most frequent overlay materials were beargrass, which was left a natural cream color or dyed yellow, and cedar bark, left a natural brown, dyed red with alder bark or dyed black with mud.

Occasionally the Twana employed a full twist when overlaying the design area just below the rim. When the weft strands were given a full twist the decorative overlay elements appeared on the inside as well as the exterior of the baskets. One weft was overlaid with beargrass and the other cedar bark. The portion of the design that was light-colored on the exterior was dark on the reverse interior side, and vice versa. This reverse color technique seems to have dropped out of the weaving repertoire in the early twentieth century.

Wrapped twining was another technique used for artistically decorated baskets. Although used extensively on open baskets, its appearance on soft twined works is relatively rare. In wrapped twining, one of the two weft strands is held rigid on the inside of the basket and bound to the warps by a flexible weft that wrapped around it. The interior and exterior of a wrapped twine basket have a different look: the wrapping weft is oriented vertically on the interior while on the outer wall it is horizontally oriented. Decoration is done through the substitution of colored strands for the wrapping weft.

PUGET SALISH

Puget Salish soft twined baskets are generally constructed in plain twining, sometimes with overlay decoration. Cedar bark commonly forms the base and cattail the warp and weft of the sides. Beargrass, plain or dyed yellow, appears as a decorative element. Designs are linear or rectangular, frequently consisting of horizontal bands of solid color or beading.

The bases of these Puget Salish baskets show a wide range of variation, including twill and checker woven cedar bark as well as plain twined cattails.

The only recorded Puget Salish name for a twined basket design is one used to describe a work of Annie Squally of Whollochet Bay, a saltwater Puyallup group, collected by Waterman. This repre-

Hattie Cush Johns, a Quilcene Twana, with symbols of wealth—a fur cape, dugout canoe, large cattail mat and soft twined baskets. Edward S. Curtis collected a number of baskets from Twana weavers Lucy (Mrs. Frank) Allen and Phoebe Charley. From E.S. Curtis, The North American Indian, vol. 9; courtesy of Historical Photography Collection, University of Washington Libraries.

sents a "place where waters of a creek trickle over something." (Waterman 1973:22) The pattern is composed of two parts. The lower element is called "very small upright objects" and consists of solid vertical stripes. The upper section, representing falling water, is a series of diagonal lines.

TWANA BASKETS (t'qayas)

A shared technology underlies the Puget Salish and Twana soft twined baskets, but the Twana developed a unique style of decoration that sets their work apart from their neighbors. The characteristic of Twana soft twined basketry is half-twist overlay in which both weft strands are covered with beargrass or cedar bark. Added to this was a set of designs which are as complex as those on Puget Sound coiled baskets. Although the reasons for such a development in one Puget Sound division

and not the other are unclear, it is known that Twana baskets have been distinct for quite some time.

A basket fragment found in a headman's quarters of an Ozette Village house, located south of Neah Bay, exhibits both overlay decoration and a distinct realistic design which greatly resembles the unique "dog" rim design found on nineteenth century Twana baskets. Since both overlay technique and realistic rim designs are rare on baskets found at Ozette, the basket was most likely obtained through a series of trades or ritual exchanges. (Croes 1979:178) The basket is tentatively dated to 1480, making it the earliest known example of the Twana "dog" tradition.

The earliest collected Twana baskets are two obtained by the Wilkes Expedition in 1841 along Hood Canal. Like the basket fragment found at Ozette, these contain "dogs" as the rim design. For main designs they have "starfish" and "salmon gills."

The shape of Twana t'qayas has remained fairly uniform from the earliest collected examples to the

Alternate direction twining with overlay. (Burke 1-1196)

Spiral twining with overlay. (WSHS B)

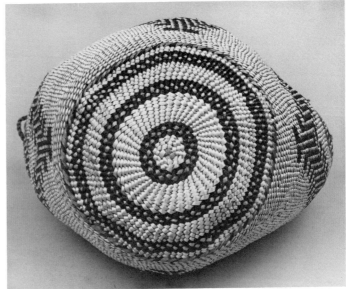

TOP—*Checker weave and plain twining. (Burke 1-1197)*
BOTTOM—*Overlaid twill. (Burke 1-505)*

Phoebe Charley with a basket showing her use of wolf and salmon gill designs. From E.S. Curtis, The North American Indian, *vol. 9; courtesy of Historical Photography Collection, University of Washington Libraries.*

present day. Typically, they have a round base, slightly flared sides, and a round mouth. The height of the sides is approximately the same as the diameter of the mouth. Some Twana baskets have shorter, straighter sides, and occasionally a very tall, narrow shape is seen. Only a few examples of a round bowl shape have been recorded, all dating from at least the early 1900s.

Older Twana baskets are apt to be considerably larger than those made in more recent years. This is due to the change in their function from storage containers for clothing and other dry household goods to items made for sale to tourists and collectors. The newer baskets, averaging 5 to 10 inches tall, with simpler designs, can be made at a faster rate, thereby providing a more steady (though small) source of income.

A number of different weaves are found on the bottoms of Twana *t'qayas*, even more than on Puget Salish soft twined examples. These weaves include plaiting (both checker and 2/2 twill), plain twining

and wrapped twining. The plain twined bottoms show several variations. They may begin with a rectangular, spiral or oval start. Decorative techniques associated with rectangular starts are alternate direction twining, where parallel rows alternate in the slant of the stitch to make patterns like chevrons, and overlay of dark cedar bark and light beargrass. This use of alternate direction twining indicates that weavers were aware of the effects of stitch slant and that the direction was not the result of right or left handedness. Overlay can also be found on the spiral twine bottoms, making concentric rows of solid or beaded lines. The spiral twine base appears most often on smaller baskets, while other methods provided the support necessary for large sizes.

Checker and 2/2 twill weaves usually form a rectangle in the center of the base, with twining around the outer portion. For extra strength, cedar root was sometimes utilized in this section. Elements could be overlaid to form decorative patterns. A rather unusual variation is a combination of checker weave and plain twining in which rows of each alternate in a square. Wrapped twining occasionally appears on the bottom of soft twined baskets, forming concentric rows of different colors. A twining technique that is found only on bottoms has the wefts criss-cross over the warps.

A bone of a deer's foreleg, tapered and sharpened to a point, was used to tighten and straighten the wefts. According to legend, this bone was the implement filed by Deer to kill *duk^{w}ibał*. Upon discovery it was placed by the Changer into the leg of the would-be assassin, Deer.

On most Twana *t'qayas* a series of adjacent loops or "ears" were added to the top. Traditionally these loops were constructed of fiber cordage and were used to tie the top of the basket closed. Since two sides were folded inward to facilitate the closure, the loops were necessarily pliable. When Twana baskets became salable items, the loops became decorative rather than functional. They were constructed of cedar roots or branches and attached with root stitches. Occasionally the single row of loops was elaborated into double or triple rows of scallop-like forms.

In addition to the linear and rectangular designs which were used by the Puget Salish on twined baskets, the Twana extended their inventory by making use of coiled designs. The "starfish" and "salmon gills" designs are good examples of this. Weavers sought to surpass each other not only in execution but also in developing new, innovative patterns. Starting with a basic rectangular design such as the Puget Salish "box," numerous variations were developed, each showing a slightly different combination of design elements. The first such was probably the creation of the Twana "box" design, with the accompanying shift of names for the original from "box" to "starfish."

The hallmark of Twana soft twined basketry is the zoomorphic rim design. The working surface of the basket is divided into two design fields, with a narrow band for the rim design and a broad main design area beneath. Rim designs typically depict "dogs," "wolves" and "helldivers." Found also are geometric figures such as "star," "mountain" and beaded stripes. Rim designs are usually separated from the main designs by one or more horizontal lines. Both design fields usually show dark patterns on a light background. On a few baskets the rim design field does not appear and the surface is treated as a single field. A rare older example displays four separate horizontal fields, a narrow band of "wolves" at the rim, a slightly wider band of "stars," a broad area of diagonal "salmon gills" and another band of "stars" near the base.

Main designs on Twana *t'qayas*, like Puget Sound coiled baskets, are arranged in a variety of ways: horizontal, vertical, diagonal and all-over. Horizontal arrangements appear frequently and consist of bands of geometric designs or rows of animal figures. The vertical orientation is the most common, generally made up of four columns, one on each side of the basket. The numerous forms based on the rectangular "box" design usually appear in fours, sometimes having filler designs of human or animal figures between the columns. Other vertical designs

such as "starfish" are positioned in equidistant rows around the basket.

The most common of diagonal arrangements are opposing diagonals, forming large vees or zig-zags. "Salmon gills" and "rainbow" usually appear in single, double or triple series of opposing diagonals. Occasionally a diagonal placement of elements slanting up to the right is seen.

It is very rare to find an all-over arrangement of designs on Twana soft twined baskets. The conventions of more organized design concepts dominate their art, despite the existence of all-over designs on Puget Sound coiled baskets.

Twana soft basket designs often varied from weaver to weaver and occasionally from basket to basket. The following section outlines designs for which names are known. Designs will be considered in groups based on design elements: zoomor-

Helldivers at the rim of a Twana basket made by Louisa Baker. (Burke 1-490)

45

phic and anthropomorphic, rectangular, triangular, linear and complex. According to weavers, all designs had names. With the loss of language and culture in the years following European contact, many of the names have been lost.

TWANA DESIGNS—Zoomorphic and Anthropomorphic

There are three main zoomorphic designs found on Twana baskets, helldiver, dog and wolf, along with the two anthropomorphic designs, man and woman.

HELLDIVER

The Twana "helldiver" is akin to animal designs to the west and south, being found among the Quinault, Upper and Lower Chehalis, Clatsop and Tillamook. For the Quinault it represents a "seagull" while for the Upper Chehalis it is an *c'ayum'*, a

Dogs with "elbowed" legs on a basket made by Satsop Anne. (SCM 1074-170)

four-legged mammal which was thought to walk along the treetops. Since the Clatsop are the only non-Salish group to have this pattern and it is not shared by others related to them, the invention appears to be of a Salish origin.

"Helldiver" is an English nickname given to the horned grebe (*Podiceps auritus*). This small fish duck was eaten as a game bird and gained its prominence through a story where it was cast as the unfaithful wife of heron. The design itself consists of a small figure with two slanted legs. The Twana version faces left, the same as the Quinault "seagull" but the opposite of the other groups. This reflects the necessary correlation between the forward slanting legs and the pitch of Twana and Quinault baskets which slant up to the right, while the others slant up to the left. When, as in one rare example, a "helldiver" faces to the right, it necessarily has straight legs.

On Twana soft twined baskets the "helldiver" is found as a sole rim design, as a "filler" with other rim design animals, and as the main design in horizontal bands.

DOG

The "dog" design is characterized by four legs and an upturned tail. Dogs existed on Puget Sound prior to European contact. The Twana kept three breeds of dogs: one used for its wool, another for hunting and one as a guard dog. (Thompson ms.) The Twana name for the design, $sq^w\partial bay$, is the generic term that encompasses all breeds.

The "dog" design has evolved over the years, most notably in its leg representation. The rim design fragment uncovered at Ozette has legs composed of three stitches on the leftward facing figure. While the hind legs are straight the lowest stitches of the front legs are positioned to the rear, giving them a look of motion, with arched "paws."

The next stage is seen on the baskets collected by the Wilkes Expedition in 1841. Here all four legs, each composed again of three stitches, slant forward on the lower stitch giving the effect of elbowed "legs." As before the "dog" faces left. This version has the visual impact of being a tighter design than the earlier one in that the final stitches are contiguous with the rest of the legs, rather than beaded.

The final stage, also predating European contact in its inception, totally replaced the "elbow-legged-look" by the end of the first third of this century. Here the four legs are straight vertical bars, again three strands long. The straight-legged "dogs" may have been developed to facilitate symmetry on main designs, since they could be woven to face either direction.

The other major change which has come about deals with the shape of the head of the "dog." The Ozette fragment exhibits a head which extends behind the neck. The head is two stitches wide and four stitches in length, with one row of those stitches set in back of the one-strand-wide neck column. One early-collected basket shows this trait as well although the legs are elbowed. By the mid-nineteenth century the style of the design had changed in that the neck column was widened to two stitches. This placement made for a flat look at the back of the head as now it was set over the newly added neck stitch.

The great variation seen in the straight-legged examples of the Twana "dog" indicates that there was never only one design at a given time but rather a most common one. The common twentieth century "dog" has a nine-stitch-long bosy. Frequent variations are found for bodies of seven and eight stitches in length. Other deviations include narrowing of the body width and curving the tail.
tury "dog" has a nine-stitch-long body. Frequent variations are found for bodies of seven and eight stitches in length. Other deviations include narrowing of the body width and curving the tail.

WOLF

The "wolf" design is based on the "dog," having the same head, neck, body and legs as the straight-legged "dog." The "dog" has an upturned tail while the "wolf" has a downward slanting tail. With the decline of the timber wolf in the area and the appearance and importance of the horse, the "wolf" was

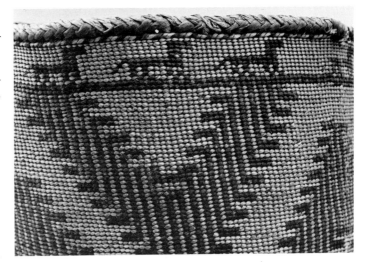

TOP—An attempt to portray wolves with "elbowed" legs. Due to the pitch of the twining, leg stitches are discontiguous. (Burke 1-498)

BOTTOM—Straight-legged dogs facing to the right, human figures below, on a basket woven by Lucy (Mrs. Frank) Allen. (WSHS T255)

reinterpreted as "horse" by some Twana after 1890. Due to the slant of the tail, the "wolf" faces toward the right in order to match the slope with the direction of the pitch.

Unlike the "dog," the "wolf" appears only rarely on coiled work. On soft twined baskets "wolves" are usually found in the role of rim designs; occasionally they are seen on the main design field. Variations include different body, head, tail and leg lengths, attempts to slant the legs, a narrowing of the head width, and a tail which goes up vertically before slanting downward.

MAN AND WOMAN

Less frequent than "dogs," "wolves" and "helldivers" are depictions of people. "Men" are portrayed far more often than "women." These designs are found on the main design field in connection with other designs, such as "fish net." Occasionally a "man," reduced in size, is found as a filler in a rim design band of animals.

Human designs were placed on Twana soft twined baskets prior to this century. The distinction between males and females rests in the latter wearing skirts, a practice which predates white contact. Unlike Puget Salish coiled human figures, Twana people are not represented with hands. Key variations are found among Twana humans in the following aspects: head and neck shape, presence or absence of feet, slanted versus perpendicular feet, and rounded versus square shoulders.

As well as a number of anomalous (and anonymous) creatures, "flounder," "deer," "mountain goat" and "seal" are also found on Twana soft twined baskets. "Flounder" and "seal" are each discussed under triangular designs in the following section. "Deer" and "mountain goat" are themselves based on the "dog" design. The "deer" faces toward the right while the "goat" faces leftward. The "deer" has ears while the "goat" has horns. The "deer's" head is down and its ears back. The "goat" has a longer tail than the short one of the "deer."

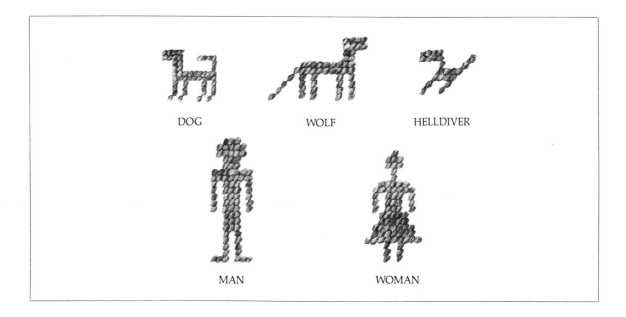

DOG   WOLF   HELLDIVER

MAN   WOMAN

MAIN DESIGNS

1. RECTANGULAR

CONCENTRIC RECTANGLES - A basic design element of Twana soft twined baskets is the rectangle with concentric lines, usually light against a dark solid or striped background. The simple "box" design has a solid rectangular center surrounded by concentric rectangles with flanges on the two vertical sides; variations of the "box" have broken lines around the center rectangle, thereby forming dark triangles or bars. These designs are usually arranged in vertical series of four columns around the basket. Within the columns they may be from one to four across.

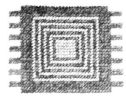

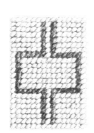

STARFISH - The "starfish" is analagous to the Puget Salish coiled basketry design "box," being a vertical series of internally connected rectangles.

STAR - Like the Puget Salish "fly" design, the "star" is composed of small squares forming a checkerboard pattern.

FISH WEIR - Vertical lines placed in a square represent the poles of a salmon weir set in a river.

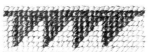

2. TRIANGULAR

MOUNTAIN - An upward pointed triangle of solid color. A single or double row of these represents a mountain range.

ICICLE - The same as "mountain" but pointing downward.

SPIDER WEB - Similar to "mountain" and "icicle" but without any solid colored triangles; a zig-zag line.

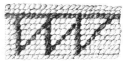

The preceding designs are found both as rim designs and as main designs in horizontal bands. Due to restrictions placed on their formation by pitch, the triangles are formed by a slanting line up to the right and a vertical line.

FLOUNDER - An equal-sided diamond representing the shape of this flat fish. It can be found between rectangles and within design complexes.

BUTTERFLY - Vertically connected triangles, usually set between vertical main designs.

LIGHTNING - A zig-zag design placed vertically at intervals around the basket. It is the same design as one called "mountain" by the Quinault.

RAINBOW - Alternating light and dark zig-zag bands running horizontally around the basket, filling the main design area. This design has been seen with dark "dogs" placed on the white bands and with light and dark "stars" over the entire field.

FLYING GEESE - Placed between horizontal bands, rows of beading zig-zag around the basket.

FISH NET - A criss-cross pattern over the entire basket which forms large diamond-shaped spaces into which human figures were sometimes placed.

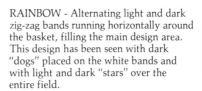

49

3. LINEAR

HANDS OR FINGERS - Short vertical lines with bars at the top, placed so that they become progressively shorter from the center. They usually number five or six; if five, the center line is shaped like a "T." This design may appear as a separate motif in open areas or in combination with other elements such as "boxes" and "crow's dishes."

SALMON GILLS - The same pattern occurs on coiled basketry throughout Puget Sound, a diagonal series of short linear segments turned outward at each end. On Twana soft twined baskets, "salmon gills" are arranged in single direction or opposing diagonals.

BACKBONE - Various linear arrangements running horizontally around the basket represent the backbone of salmon, sturgeon and halibut.

HAIL - Beaded diagonals depicting falling hail.

CANES - Diagonal and vertical lines of dark and light alternate in blocks within horizontal bands, perhaps representing a doctor's staff.

SEAL ROOST - The most elaborate of all design complexes, it is based on two adjacent sets of concentric squares. The squares, with two short marks in the center of each, are "rocks." The fringe around the rectangle is "seaweed." The three triangles midway on each external length of the squares plus the diamond in the center (formed by back-to-back triangles) represent "seals" resting on the "rocks." Beneath each square are two pairs of dark vertical lines, the two outer ones having short bars attached to them. These are two harpoons, each with a hook.

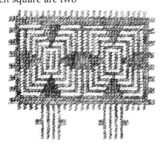

4. DESIGN COMPLEXES

Design complexes are composed of more than one named part. Often the individual parts are given a different identity than when they occur in other contexts. For example, a triangle can be called a "seal" in one design complex and a "window" in another. All design complexes appear to be based on rectangular backgrounds.

CROW'S FEET AND DISHES - Stacked trapezoids with "hand" designs inside, "crow's feet." Crow is a frequent character in Puget Sound lore, used in explaining geographic features and saltwater shell forms. "Crow dishes" (keyhole limpets found at a site south of Lilliwaup called "crow's fishtrap") were strung together and worn as a necklace. The trapezoids represent their shape.

FLOUNDER IN A BOX - A diamond, the "flounder," is positioned at the center of a set of concentric rectangles. This is probably a rendition of the flat fish placed in a container after being caught.

PUPPY - The two-legged animal, which otherwise is called "helldiver," when placed inside a diamond within a rectangle is interpreted as a "puppy."

HOUSE - Concentric rectangles broken by a triangle placed midway on the base and pointing to the center. The window, represented by the triangle, was said to have been made of cattail matting.

PLATE NO. 7

PLATE NO. 8

53

PLATE NO. 10

PLATE NO. 9

PLATE NO. 11

54

PLATE NO. 12

PLATE NO. 13

PLATE NO. 14

PLATE NO. 15

PLATE NO. 16

PLATE NO. 17

PLATE NO. 18

PLATE NO. 20

PLATE NO. 21

PLATE NO. 22   PLATE NO. 23

58

PLATE NO. 26.

PLATE NO. 27

60

PLATE NO. 28

PLATE NO. 30

PLATE NO. 29

PLATE No. 31

PLATE No. 32   PLATE No. 33

PLATE NO. 34

PLATE NO. 35

PLATE NO. 36

PLATE NO. 37

PLATE NO. 38

PLATE NO. 40

PLATE NO. 41

PLATE No. 42

PLATE No. 43

66

PLATE NO. 44

PLATE NO. 45

PLATE NO. 46

PAGE NO. 47

68

PLATE NO. 48

69

Descriptions of Plates

PAGE NO. 51

1. Nisqually - Coiled with full imbrication   WSHS I 353
Main Design: salmon gills
Rim Design: flies
Materials: cedar root with beargrass and horsetail root imbrication
Bottom Construction: meander
Height: 10 inches
Base Diameter: 6 x 5 inches
Collected by: Mrs. W.B. Blackwell

PAGE NO. 52

2. Puget Sound - Coiled with full imbrication   Burke 1-700
Type: child's berry basket
Main Design: stripes
Rim Design: rectangles
Materials: cedar root with beargrass, wild cherry bark and dyed cedar bark imbrication
Bottom Construction: spiral
Stitch Count: 5 warps/inch; 5 wefts/inch
Height: 3¾ inches
Base Diameter: 2½ inches
Rim Diameter: 4½ inches
Collected by: W.M. Snyder, pre-1910

3. Twana - Coiled with imbrication   Burke 1-11202
Type: child's berry basket
Main Design: stripes
Rim Design: horizontal stripe
Materials: cedar root with beargrass and dyed cedar bark imbrication
Bottom Construction: meander
Stitch Count: 3 warps/inch; 7 wefts/inch
Height: 4 inches
Base Diameter: 3 inches
Rim Diameter: 4¾ inches
Collected by: F.C. Shirtleff, ca. 1890

4. Puget Sound - Coiled with full imbrication   SCM 76-24-4
Main Design: snake in black on white
Materials: cedar root with beargrass and horsetail root imbrication
Bottom Construction: meander
Height: 9½ inches
Base Diameter: 5¼ x 6 inches
Rim Diameter: 8⅝ inches

5. Puyallup - Coiled with full imbrication   WSHS I 279
Main Design: boxes
Materials: cedar root with beargrass and horsetail root imbrication
Bottom Construction: meander
Stitch Count: 4 warps/inch; 6 wefts/inch
Height: 12⅞ inches
Base Diameter: 8 inches
Rim Diameter: 15¾ inches
Collected by: Mrs. W.B. Blackwell

6. Nisqually - Coiled with full imbrication   Burke 1-205
Type: shallow bowl
Main Design: four triangular units with stepped edges in yellow, brown, black, white
Materials: cedar root with beargrass, cedar bark and horsetail root imbrication
Bottom Construction: spiral with beading
Stitch Count: 3 warps/inch; 6 wefts/inch
Height: 5 inches
Base Diameter: 5¼ inches
Rim Diameter: 8½ inches
Collected by: Mrs. Oda Roberts

Explanation of abbreviations
WSHS—Washington State Historical Society
SCM—State Capitol Museum (Washington State)